Music
in the
Home

Singing out *together* with your kids

by Christopher Vuk

Printed in the the Good ol' U S of A

First Printing, 2019

ISBN 9781073322633

Christopher Vuk
535 Cambridge St.
Cambridge, MA 02141
www.christophervuk.com
@christophertvuk

CONTENTS

Foreword

When Chris asked me to write the foreword to his book, I felt blessed and privileged because I've seen a remarkable transformation both in his life and business. Through Chris, this book represents the power of God and the direction He gives us in in our lives, and how He rewards us by being obedient to His Word.

Chris relies upon current conditions, his own experiences, and the wisdom of other professionals. The uniqueness of his approach, however, is the manner in which he frames his story of creative and imaginative teaching. He'll show you the five love languages of children with easy steps to follow along. It's a book and workbook all in one.

I can only hope you'll take time to learn from his journey. Interestingly enough, this book began working its magic before it was even published.

Chris is a true "music man." He started playing the violin at age six, went to Berklee College of Music, created the Boston Music Festival and Cambridge Arts Festivals, and was the Music Director of the Boston String Quartet.

And with no surprise, Chris founded and is the current CEO, of Rock and Roll Daycare.

The real challenge our schools face is whether they can

provide a new educational environment that is much richer in approach and more beneficial to the children. Chris' book encompasses and promotes diversity with classroom teaching and home practicing. These tools stimulate children and help them learn more about the world we live in and how we might make it better.

"Music can change the world because music changes people" — *Bono*

Chris' view is that the science of teaching entails the application of craft knowledge such as planning and delivering instruction. He shows that the best teachers can integrate these two forms – the aspects of craft knowledge in the heart of teaching – and in the process can create the best learning environment.

His aim is to take classrooms to another level; thereby, elevating and expanding the role of the teacher from a manager to a professional who connects with students in a way that brings inspiration and life to the teacher and child alike.

However, this book is presented in a uniquely personal way. It's "half time" and your turn to take over the responsibilities as a role model for the children under your care and have fun while doing it.

Most parents will readily say that their children are the most important thing in their lives. But many of those same people struggle to meaningfully engage with their children. For some, it's an issue of not having time and for others, it's about a lack of connection points.

The author provides appropriate detailed guidelines about how best to approach many of the required practices associated with creating a successful learning environment in the home. Then, parents are more equipped to offer hope, determination and inspiration to their children.

Music taps into people's dormant emotions and unexplainable feelings of excitement, peace, and ecstasy. Music teaches your brain to have multiple compartments that independently work together. It decreases depression, anxiety, and stress; boosts immune-system functioning; and improves physical health. Learning accompanied by music can accelerate memorization, creativity, dexterity, rationalization and can have positive life-changing benefits.

I think music in itself is healing. It's an explosive expression of humanity. It's something we are all touched by. No matter what culture we're from, everyone loves music. — *Billy Joel*

The Reprise

Do you remember the song, "Cat's in The Cradle" by Harry Chapin, about a Dad too busy in his career, that he didn't have time for his son? That could have been me.

One Christmas, when my son, Sean, was nine years old, I bought him a basketball hoop. It had to be assembled, so we went outside with our tools and put it together. During our assembly, my cell phone must have rung a dozen times until I finally turned it off. I was tempted to answer it, even though it was Christmas. After all, I make a living on the phone dealing with clients. But I resisted the temptation, and Sean and I played basketball for hours. I know because by the end, I was exhausted.

Afterward, Sean said to me, "This was my favorite day, Dad." I said, "Really? Why? Because it's Christmas?" "No," he said. I asked, "Because you got a basketball hoop?" "No," he replied again.

"Then why?" I asked.

With a smile on his face, he said, "Because I know how important your phone calls are, yet I must be more important, because you didn't even answer one call when you were with me."

It brings tears to my eyes when I recall how much it meant to him to have my undivided attention. My boy's greatest gift was the time I spent with him that day.

"Timing is everything" in life!
— Bobby DelVecchio

The time to absorb this book is now, and the processes it employs, giving your child the competitive edge in realizing their absolute full potential.

by: Bobby DelVecchio
Consultant. Author. Musician.
(former drummer for Dick Clark, Chuck Berry, Bo Diddley, Chubby Checker, The Shirelles, The Dovels, Jackie Wilson, The Coasters, The Drifters, Gary U.S. Bonds, Gene Pitney, The Edgar Winter Group.)

Introduction

Kids aren't fun.

I think that often (and yes, I'm writing a book about kids, while most of my adult life has been spent working with kids … I also have four kids).

When my two-year-old twins were screaming in the back of my van for 30 minutes straight, it wasn't fun.

When my four-year-old son hasn't fallen asleep yet after lying in bed with him forever, and it's midnight, that's not fun.

I'm also terrible at arts and crafts (I seem to have skipped that class in school), and when my daughter asks if we can do an art project together … no … it's not that fun.

Some of my favorite memories of my father during childhood were playing basketball together. While it didn't happen much, I never forgot it (maybe it was also because he had no idea what to do, and he looked like a complete... well... Dad, if you're reading this, sorry!). He never watched basketball, and didn't care for sports in general, although he never had a problem with me playing. I don't think playing basketball with me would have been on his top 10 list, but when he saw me outside playing by myself, he realized that it was something that he and I could do together.

Most parents will readily say that their children are the most important thing in their lives (what about your spouses, people?). But many, if not most, of those same people struggle to meaningfully engage with their children. For some, it's an issue of not having time and for others, it's about a lack of connection points.

What do you do when your child loves playing with dolls, but you always hated them as a child?

No, it's not a rhetorical question (although I do love the word, "rhetorical"). If your kid wants to play dolls, stop what you're doing and play dolls with her. Sure, you don't have to do it every time, but trust is so important in the life of a child (and when is it not important as an adult, either?). You want your child to believe and trust you will be there when she calls for you if she's hurt or if she just wants to play Barbie.

Sometimes we still struggle, though. Maybe your kids don't want to play dolls or LEGOs with you. How can you engage with them then, if it sometimes feels like they don't want you around?

I'm a music guy. I started the violin at age six, went to school for music, had a career playing music, and eventually, started a business teaching people how to make music. So, understandably, my answer is all about music. And that's what this book is all about.

Music is a team sport, and though some may argue against it, all are equipped to play it (if you're highlighting, start with that sentence).

Part of our humanity is wrapped up in music. It must say something about us as a species when some of the most expensive items on our planet are pieces of art, or the instruments of its creation.

We, as people, bond together around music. Rarely will you find someone who doesn't like music. While our specific tastes may differ, we all desire to gather around the same table.

And so, this book is my invitation to you, the reader, to gather with others and partake in music together.

Musical or non-musical, tonal or tone-deaf, I've written this for you. I hope that these pages inspire you and lead you to action. At the end of each chapter, I've included a *challenge*. I encourage you to complete the *challenge* in your book. Some *challenges* will require you to do something before you write about

> **66 Music is a team sport, and all are equipped to play it. 99**

them, and others you can complete right away.

I invite you to throw away your preconceptions about what can or cannot be done and open up your imagination to possibility.

Why your kid
hates piano lessons…
and what to do about it

Why your kid hates piano lessons…

and what to do about it

Practice makes perfect … right? Well, kinda, sorta, maybe. It depends.

I have a 4-year-old drummer and a 6-year-old violinist turned pianist, and I've seen my share of tears and grumpy faces.

I'm a professional violinist, but I seem to have forgotten somewhere along the way all the poking and prodding that my mom did to get me to practice when I was a kid. But now that I'm doing all the poking and prodding to my kids, I think I understand why my mom was tired so often…

Has your child ever told you they love brushing their teeth, studying for a test, or eating green vegetables? Now, before you accuse me of comparing practicing the piano to brushing your teeth, let me tell you that that's exactly what I'm going to do.

Practicing is boring. It's not that fun. And that's okay.

There's no hard and fast rule that states that everything in a child's life must be fun. Math isn't fun for most people (and if you find my comment offensive because you like math, then keep it to yourself and just read). But there's no getting around that class unless you go to music college (like I did). And just so there's no judgement here, I am incredible at adding and subtracting.

Practice doesn't have to be the best part of your child's day, and as a parent you shouldn't feel guilty about making your child practice (I'm sure there are other books on parenting that can lower your self esteem). Sure, maybe you have some kind of practice or goal chart that your child works towards every week, and if they practice a certain amount of hours they get a special treat, like ice cream, or movie/video game time. The experts say not to overdo it and that children should develop intrinsic motivation, but if your kids practice an hour or two every day so they can play Warcraft for 30 minutes (that's a video game for those of you who were born before 1980), I'd say it's a pretty fair trade.

❝You don't need to feel guilty about making your child practice❞

When I was a teenager, I went to a summer camp in the woods where if you didn't practice five hours every day, they would kick you out of camp (yes, total nerd).

Practice has to be routine. It has to be consistent. In our house, practice begins at 7:15 am every day. It's not a surprise, it's a fact. You're not surprised you have school each weekday, you know you've just gotta be there. I'm all for making practice a gateway to other things. My folks always had a rule about practicing before I could play, and I'll tell you what, I made sure I practiced every day.

For beginners and young children in particular, the parent really must get involved from the start. A four-year-old does not understand what to do with a violin (or any instrument for that matter). Trust me, I've worked with plenty of them. Some things are intuitive, like many sports. It doesn't take a beautiful mind to realize that a basketball belongs in a hoop. It does take a genius, however, to understand how to draw a bow across a violin string without seeing it done a few thousand times.

But remember, private lessons are helpful only so far as the parent reinforces what has been learned at home.

So, before you tell me that all this is impossible for a working mom or dad to do, consider the time investment. If you want your child to develop a basic musical competency on an instrument, like many parents do, then spending five minutes out of the day sitting down with them to practice, will do it. What I have learned from my own children is that while practicing with them is essential, you can also overdo it. And so, while I practice with my kids every day, I try to give them space to practice on their own as well.

What that looks like for me, with a pianist and a drummer at home is that the 6-year-old starts practicing piano on her own while I sit down with my 4-year-old son at the drums. After five minutes or so, I leave him to practice on his own, and I sit down to work with my daughter for a while. After I'm done, they both usually practice a little bit more on their own.

Don't be intimidated by the whole "I don't know how to play an instrument," or "I'm tone deaf" excuse. Introductory music books are pretty good and provide the basics for anyone to get started. YouTube has a staggering number of videos to learn about anything (music included), and if you're really struggling (or just want to take things to the next level), get a music teacher involved. They'd be happy to take your money.

Bottom line is that your kid is probably not going to be motivated to practice on their own (just accept it). As a parent, you will need to take the road less traveled by. And that will make all the difference (Robert Frost anyone)? Anyway, practice with your kid and you'll be fine.

CHALLENGE #1

Well, the challenge for this chapter is a no brainer.
Practice with your kid and write about it.
Maybe you'll even have fun. Toodles.

_____

_____

_____

_____

_____

_____

_____

_____

_____

_____

_____

_____

_____

What non-musical parents can teach their kids about music

CHAPTER TWO

What non-musical parents
can teach their kids
about music

If there's one word I hate, it's got to be the word "talent."

I hear parents all the time say things like, "He's not talented enough for that," or "Those other kids are so talented" or "I was never talented"

I disagree and science doesn't agree either.

Malcolm Gladwell, who wrote the New York Times Bestseller, *Outliers*, popularized the idea which states that any person who spends 10,000 hours on a specific activity will become a master at it. In a new book, *Peak*, by psychologists Anders Ericsson and Robert Pool, they argue that except for height and body size,

the key to extraordinary performance is thousands and thousands of hours of hard, focused work.

Have you ever heard someone say, "Oh, he's not talented enough to learn algebra," or "Her mother and I can't spell, so she probably can't either."

No! That's crazy. Your child's teacher would laugh you out of the room.

So, why do we accept answers like that about music education? Why don't we do what lots of parents do with their kid when he or she is struggling with math or spelling? Why don't we just learn it with them?

Woah, woah, wait now. You're probably thinking to yourself, I used to know how to do math, and I think I know how to spell, but I never knew how to play music.

Ok, fair point. Let me give you a quick test.

Say your alphabet from A to G.

Count to four.

Clap your hands.

Did you do it? If you did… Congratulations! You too can learn music.

All right, let's get to it. If you've never learned music, what can you actually do with your child? A lot! Let's check it out. I'll start easy, and then I'll progress to more advanced stuff for those parents that are a little bit more ambitious.

❶ Listen to music together. It doesn't get much easier than that. Turn on some music in your car. Put some music on at home. You can even watch music videos (be smart here people!). But don't leave it there. Talk about it. Was it fast or slow, happy or sad? How did it make you feel? Do you want to dance or take a nap (most parents I know would vote for a nap!).

❷ Learn about musicians or composers and listen to their music. Did you know that most college students go through a course called Music Appreciation? And do you know what they do in that course (this is really hard, so you might want to stop and think about it for a moment)? They learn about music (gasp!). Okay, okay, it's a bit more than that. They actually learn about musicians or composers and listen to their music (not to diss those college professors, but parents, you've got a smartphone...right?). Stop by the library and get a book or research online. Show your kids what the music of Mozart sounds like and how it was inspired by his lifestyle in Vienna. Or check out some of Michael Jackson's songs and learn how to moonwalk with your kids (honestly, what kid doesn't want to learn how to moonwalk?).

❸ Get a music app for your device. But, use the program along with your child. I've seen plenty of kids using "educational apps" and it just turns into TV time. Help them

engage with the program and
ask them questions about it.
Learn how to play the game
yourself (adults can play video games too, right?).

4 **Get a children's songbook.** When I started
Fiddlefox Music, I wanted to create children's songbooks that
would teach children about music from around the world.
When you pick up a songbook (and mine are the best...just
sayin'), make sure that you have some kind of audio recording
that goes with it (unless you were a vocal performance major
in college). Singing songs together is one of my kid's favorite
bedtime activities.

5 **Playing musical games is another great activity.**
This works well with a songbook. If you're singing a song about
a train, pretend you're riding in circles together on the train.
You can sing the song fast and slow, loud and soft, high and low.
A little research will give you a lot of ideas for easy things that
you can do.

6 **Finally, prepare on your own.** This will probably
connect more with Do-it-Yourself parents in the audience,
but what's to stop you from learning a few rhythm patterns on
your own, and practicing them with your child later? Or from
learning a song by yourself, and then teaching it to your little
one. They'll think you're brilliant, which you are, of course!

Parents are the greatest, underutilized resource for creating the next generation of musical kids.

You hold your child's potential in your hands (didn't Uncle Ben say something to Peter Parker about that? With great power comes great…). Don't be afraid to make mistakes though; it's inevitable. Try new things. If you're learning something new, show it to your child, and work on it together. You're only limited by your own imagination.

CHALLENGE #2

I'd like you to pick an activity from the list and do it with your kid. Write about which activity you chose, and what happened when you worked on it with your child(ren). **Tell me if you thought it was easy to do or hard.**

1. Listen to music together
2. Learn about musicians or composers and listen to their music
3. Get a music app for your device
4. Get a children's songbook to use
5. Play a musical game together
6. Finally, prepare on your own and share

_____

_____

_____

_____

_____

_____

_____

I accidentally did this,
and it's a lifesaver for families
with multiple kids

CHAPTER THREE

I accidentally did this, and it's a lifesaver for families with multiple kids

As the parent of four children under the age of six, I'm constantly looking for ways to balance my time. (You can relate, right?) You play LEGOs with one, toss the ball around with the other, play dress up with the little princess, while the older boy wants a story. And so, you (like the good parent you are) go around and try to spend time with each child. And sometimes it works. But then the phone rings, or a friend stops by, you get called into the office, or suddenly it's bedtime, and you haven't played with little Johnny. So what question do we, as parents, ask ourselves? Am I a good parent?

Well, first, the idea of balance is nonsense, so chuck that out the window and get rid of your guilt.

Psychology shows that children don't need equal time with their parents.

Wait a second. *What?*

Yes, that controversial thing I just said is true. Children do not need equal time with Mom or Dad. Some kids feel love when you hug and kiss them, others feel loved when you give them gifts, or serve and help them, encourage them, and yes some (but not all!) children feel love the most when you spend time with them.

If you want to learn more, check out Gary Chapman's book, ***The 5 Love Languages of Children.***

So, if balancing your time with your children becomes less of a problem, what does that mean for us as parents (more time for naps, maybe)? It means you need not force your kids to play with you. If you've invited your daughter to play a game with you, and she doesn't want to, don't sweat it. Ask your son, or one of your other children. The trick here is to keep on offering. If she doesn't want to play today, it doesn't mean she won't want to do it tomorrow, or the next day, just keep asking. You can also follow her interests and ask her what she would like to do with you.

Parents, your kids are brilliant! Sometimes you just need to be

#brilliantkids

quiet, and listen to what they're telling you, because they usually will. When I started Fiddlefox Music, I asked myself repeatedly how to develop a music program that would be exciting for children, and help them learn about the music, people, and cultures of the world.

What I found amazed me, but I couldn't believe I didn't see it before. Have you ever watched what happens to children when you turn up the music really loud? First thing that usually happens is that the children stop what they're doing and gather around the source of the sound. My kids have actually gotten up on stage with the band a few times.... awkward... Then, something incredible occurs. They dance.

It's not planned or pre-constructed. They just wiggle their bodies around to the music. And what is even more remarkable is that many children will move to the beat of the music and sing along to the lyrics regardless of the language it's in.

Unfortunately, for many, if not most parents, this is where it ends. We look at the kids, and say *"that's so cute"* take a picture on our phones, and then sit down to check our email. Now, don't get all self-righteous on me now. We've all done it. I've done it. But you're reading this because you want to learn how to be better.

What would you say if your child brought home an A+ on their calculus test? I'm doubting that many of you would say

"Aww, that's soo cute" No! You would probably say something like, *"Let's celebrate and go out to a nice restaurant tonight or go to the movies!"* So why do we treat the accomplishments of young children so differently?

Let me describe it more scientifically. A two-year-old child spontaneously begins to rhythmically move their body at a consistent frequency while altering their vocal chords to produce a sound in alignment in timbre, pitch, and enunciation with that of another person. Are you impressed now? Would you rather take that kid out for dinner and a movie?

66 Why do we treat the accomplishments of young children so differently? 99

I'm not here to boost restaurant and box office sales, but I want to help you see that your kids can do amazing things! Spontaneous dance parties like this are one of the greatest single activities you can do together as a family (well, that and eating ice cream, of course).

Dance parties are one guaranteed activity that kids won't want to miss out on. If you and your spouse are up there dancing like there is no tomorrow (and yes, in my mind that is the *only* way to dance), then your kids will not only be mesmerized into thinking *"That's my dad??"* or *"I never knew Mom could move like that!"* They'll come and join you.

I accidentally did this, and it's a lifesaver for families with multiple kids **31**

I've seen this time after time. No kid wants to miss out on a good time. And if you're a parent with multiple kids that wants to get that time in with every kid, I can't think of a better way to do it. The great thing about music is that you can always change it. Listen to different types of music, do free dance, or make up your own dance moves. Dance in a circle holding hands, or dance by yourselves.

If you or your kids can play an instrument, play along with the recording, or have some people play instruments and some people dance. Get in there and have fun. And if you really want to impress your kids, practice a dance move beforehand and show them the move while the music is playing. I'm sure that your kids will think you're amazing!

I accidentally did this, and it's a lifesaver for families with multiple kids

CHALLENGE #3

Now that you've heard me talk about dancing,
I'd like you to go out and have a dance party with
your kids. Once you've done it, write about it below.
What did your kids think about it as well?

_____

_____

_____

_____

_____

_____

_____

_____

_____

_____

_____

_____

_____

Can't sing?

Here's an easy step for parents

towards musical literacy

Can't sing?

Here's an easy step for parents
towards musical literacy

Do you need to know how to read music? Nope.

Do you need to know how to play an instrument? Not required.

Do you need to know how to find "C" on the piano? Not unless you're a pirate (sorry…preschool humor, please forgive me).

You may not be musical, but all parents can learn music with their children.

The Suzuki method has become one of the most popular methods for teaching music around the world. Developed by Shinichi Suzuki during the 20th century, the Suzuki method has also been called the "Mother-Tongue" Approach.

What Suzuki did that was so revolutionary is that he took the way that we all learn our first language, English, Japanese, Russian, and he applied it to music. Suzuki famously said that *all Japanese children speak Japanese*. Well, of course they do! Their moms and dads, grandparents, cousins, and friends all speak to them in their native language. And the children learn it naturally. Let's stop there and think about music now.

Most kids I've observed like to sing. So, how do you learn how to sing? You do it by hanging out with people who are singing.

> 66 Suzuki famously said that all Japanese children speak Japanese. 99

How do you learn to play the violin? By hanging out with people who play the violin.

Now, I know you're thinking, but I don't know anybody that plays the violin. Well, find them! It's not like they're hiding (although, they might be in a stuffy practice room). Most, actually, want to be found.

Now, I want to be clear, I'm not saying you must take lessons from these people. You can, but that's not absolutely necessary at this stage. So, what do you do after you've found this music person? Simple. Get to know them. **Ask them why they wanted to learn to sing, or play the violin**. Find out how they learned to play. If they have recordings, listen to them. Ask them who else they would recommend listening to. See if they have upcoming performances, and if not, if they have any friends who have a concert you could attend.

See how this is different than what most people do? What do people do when they want to learn a musical instrument? They usually hire a music teacher, or they watch videos on YouTube. Having run a music school for seven years with over 1,000 students, I can tell you that private lessons for adults have little long-term benefits.

Sure, you might learn something after six months, but then you get busy, have another child, move to a new city, forget about it for years, and then when you decide to recommit (new year's resolution, perhaps?) you need to start all over again. I've seen it happen with most adults (and yes, I meant to use the word "most") who take music lessons.

What I'm suggesting that you do instead is to make a friend who is good at playing whatever instrument you're interested in learning. And maybe later on you actually hire this person to give you some tips or lessons and that's fine, but make sure the relationship works first.

The music student I've had for the longest period of time is a brilliant web guy. I've been working with him for about 10 years. Honestly, he's never been a very consistent student, but we developed a friendship over several years. He attended several of my concerts, I performed at some special events for him, he would send me emails about the pieces he was working on, and we still meet up to have coffee every once and a while.

Is he going to be a professional musician?

Unlikely.

Is he going to continue to get better at his instrument and love doing it?

Absolutely!

And I bet that when he has children someday, those kids will catch the excitement he had, and I can see them spending a lot of time exploring and learning music together.

CHALLENGE #4

I'd like you to find someone who plays an instrument that you'd like to learn something about. You may already know this person, and if not, do a Google search. It's easier than you think. Ask them if they have a concert you could go to, or if they would be available to meet up to talk about music over coffee. Make a friend. And don't be afraid to bring your kids. This experience will get even better if you bring them along. **Once you've done it, write about what you learned.**

_____

_____

_____

_____

_____

_____

_____

_____

Is my child talented?
and other
cringeworthy questions...

CHAPTER FIVE

Is my child talented?
and other
cringeworthy questions...

Every music teacher hates the question. How can you even try to answer it when a parent looks up to you with their hope-filled eyes, ready to hang on to every word you say, and asks:

"Is my child talented?"

> **"** How good does a kid really need to be... **"**

No! Please, parents don't do it. Don't abuse your child's teacher like that.

"Did he memorize the new song" "How's her intonation" or even the non-question that every parent seems to feel compelled to ask at the end of each lesson, "So, how'd he do today?" Any of these are okay, but "Is my child talented?" Mom and Dad, don't take yourself down that dark, lonely road.

Ok, so maybe I'm being a bit dramatic, but when we throw

around words like *talented, gifted, prodigy,* and my absolute favorite one, *wunderkind,* what exactly do we mean? How good does a kid really need to be at playing the piano to be a genius?

And how does age work into it as well? If my daughter hasn't played a musical instrument before the age of 5, did I rob her of the ability to be the next Franz Lizst or Lang Lang? There must be rules to this, right?

As you may expect, the answer is a bit more elusive than that, however, in some ways it's not.

Let's uncover basic facts to begin with.

#bodystructure

First, your body structure is crucial. There's a reason that the Boston Marathon is continuously dominated by men and women from Kenya and Ethiopia. Their lifestyle, bone structure, and "bird like" physique gives them a physical advantage over other long-distance runners.

You don't see a lot of short people in the NBA. If you're trying to put the ball in a 10-foot-tall basketball hoop, the easiest way to get there would be by having a body that is naturally closer to the net.

Look sometimes at the size of the hands on some famous string players. They're huge, and it's no accident (just for fun, do a Google search for celebrity violinist, Itzhak Perlman's hands...sounds kind of creepy when I write it down like that). Things like long fingers, bone structure, or genetics aren't attributes you can develop, they are what they are.

And scientifically speaking, this is really the first step to defining talent. But as we know, not every tall kid is a great basketball player, so there's probably more to it.

So, you can't change genetics; although, many people are trying ("Alexa, I'd like a bone extension, please"). However, what you can do is develop things like stamina, strength, and flexibility. Think about that tall basketball player again. What if his friend learned how to jump higher than him, or what if a violinist with small hands learned how to stretch their fingers further, and what if, what if?

Some physical attributes can be changed, and others cannot. Talented people learn the difference between the two, and work on the ones they can change.

Second, there is a direct relationship between how good you are at something and the amount of time you invest learning it. Everyone's got that one friend who studied abroad for a semester and came back with perfect Spanish or French, or whatever. When you ask them how they did it, they always say, "You've got to immerse yourself in the culture."

Well, for someone who has spent a lot of time living in other cultures, and can't speak a second language, I can say that's baloney. What your friend is actually doing though, and probably spending a lot of time on, is practicing speaking a second language to a variety of native speakers.

Could you do that back in your home country? Probably. Would you do it? Probably not.

> 66 Most of us don't believe kids can do incredible things. 99

You get good at doing something by practicing it. And you get great at it by practicing it a lot (wow, thanks Captain obvious!).

So why do child prodigies blow our minds? Because most of us, if we're honest about it, don't believe kids can do incredible things.

Now, now, before you get all defensive, I'll admit, most adults could probably name a few famous kids who'd they describe as incredibly talented (get on YouTube...but watch out for those cat videos!) However, when they think about the "regular" kids in their neighborhood or at their kid's school, they think, "probably not."

So, grab your calculator for a moment, and follow along.

Let's take the average kid who attends music college at age 18. He had to audition to get into music school, so he's probably pretty good, and likely the best musician amongst the hundreds or thousands of kids in his high school.

Now, let's say he started at age 7, a pretty common age to start a musical instrument. In elementary school, it's all about consistency, so we tell the kids that they only need to practice 15 minutes a day and they'll do alright.

So, 15 minutes a day or .25 hours x 365 days in a year = 91.25 hours in a year. Let's round up and call it a hundred. Elementary school is 6 years long, so 100 x 6 = 600 hours practiced while in elementary school. Not bad, eh?

Now, middle school is more serious, so let's double the daily time to 30 minutes or .5 hours. Again times 365 days in a year is 182.5 multiplied by 2 years in middle school = 365. So, now with elementary and middle school, he's up to about 1000 hours.

Here comes high school. Now we've got youth orchestra, contests, college auditions, so he's really got to work. Let's bump it up dramatically to 2 hours a day. So, 2 multiplied by 365 = 730 x 4 years = 2920. Let's call it 3000 + the 1600 hours from elementary and middle school, and we have 4600 hours practiced before high school for an average music school freshman. Pretty good, but it's a far cry from Malcolm Gladwell's 10,000-hour theory.

Now, let's bring in the child prodigy. They're much more likely to start earlier and practice more, so let's see what that could look like.

A child starts at age 3 practicing 2 hours a day. 2 x 365 = 730

Next year at 4 years old, Mom and Dad bump it up to 3 hours a day, 3 x 365 = 1095

At 5 and 6 years old, she's doing 4 hours a day, 4 x 365 x 2 = 2920

And so by her 7th birthday, this kid has practiced 4745 hours. That's over 145 hours more than our example of the college freshman.

And so, if you're surfing YouTube one day and you come across a 6-year-old piano player playing a Tchaikovsky piano concerto, Miles Davis, or Cole Porter, and you're wondering to yourself how God has graced the earth with such talent as this, Stop! Get out your calculator and do the math.

Now before you ask me who in the world is subjecting their kids to such cruel and unusual punishment as making a 4-year-old child practice music for 3 hours a day, spend a bit of time doing your research, and you'll discover that I'm not making this up.

Admittedly, I'm giving a highly simplified version of all this. Mental process, which is still a biological function, plays a role, as does the child's level of maturity, who their teacher is, and what kind of role the parent plays in developing the child's talent.

There is no formula and there is no guarantee.

Burnout is a common occurrence among children with physical and mental prowess pushed to achieve an elite status. So, be careful, people.

CHALLENGE #5

If you're inspired, intrigued, or just plain curious, I challenge you to find 3 or 4 videos of musical child prodigies on YouTube under the age of seven and watch them with your kids. **Ask them what they think, write it down.**

_____

_____

_____

_____

_____

_____

_____

_____

_____

_____

_____

_____

_____

_____

How to raise
a musical prodigy
... *safely*

How to raise a musical prodigy ... *safely*

Several years ago, a group of filmmakers created a shocking documentary based on several winners of the Queen Elizabeth International Violin Competition, which is arguably the most prestigious violin competition in the world. The documentary focused on the winners a few years after their victories. The majority of individuals in the film had either quit the violin, lost all their money, or were homeless and living out of their car.

This bothered me a lot.

Think about the most talented kid you know and fast-forward 15 years. Imagine that he gave up his dreams and he's now working a dead-end job and struggling to make ends meet at home. No family or hope for the future.

It's depressing, right? Especially when it happens to the best of us.

Well, I apologize, this is getting a bit dark. But I've seen this happen, and parents, we must be more than just careful. We must be knowledgeable.

So, if I haven't scared you off yet, let me talk to those of you parents who have some ambitious plans.

First off, it's hard for a child to become a musician without having music in their home. Kids love to mimic the behavior of others. Ever wonder why your daughter wants to sweep the floor, fix lunch, or take out the laundry? It's because she sees you doing those things and wants to be like you. Does your son dress up like Batman (mine does)? It's not because he wants to look like a child-sized bat, it's because he sees the amazing things Batman is doing, and he wants to do them too.

66 Inspire your kids with music. 99

So, inspire your kids with music. Listen to different musicians or bands. Watch videos of musicians on YouTube, or even take your kids to a concert. But do these things together. Engagement is powerful here. Talk about what they're hearing, seeing, and what they like and don't like. Otherwise, you miss so much value.

Once you've inspired your child, he may express interest in learning a musical instrument. If he's younger than 9-years-old, then violin, guitar, piano, or drums are probably the best instruments for him. Enroll him in private lessons and learn the instrument with him.

To be clear, I'm not saying you must become a great guitarist, but initially, you must know enough to help guide them at home. It's hard for a child to learn the basics of a new instrument, and many parents have bleeding eardrums from the pain it can cause (I'm joking … but, am I really?).

Parents often complain about how long it takes for their child to learn how to play an instrument, and especially when they aren't able to help them. Imagine if your daughter was trying to learn how to count, but you didn't know what a number was (am I striking a chord here)?

Educate yourself so you can help out your child.

Learn alongside them during their first months so you know what they are being taught and can help them through the process.

If you're really set on developing your child into a great musician, you must start them when they're young (I suggest before the age of six). They will require significant support from a parent at home. On the bright side, once they've figured out the basics, they'll develop a level of independence and the learning process will begin to speed up (as well as free up your time).

Now, here comes the controversy. People often ask me, "How long should my child practice each day?" Or another similar question, "What should I do if my child doesn't want to practice?"

This question should be determined by what kind of outcome you are looking for. If you want your kid to casually understand music, then it's a different answer than if you want to give your child the chance to be a great performer.

Let me rephrase the question in a few different ways. "What should you do if your child doesn't want to do his homework?" or "How much time should your child spend preparing for a test?"

The desired outcome will determine what is required. And if the outcome you want is excellence, then it requires lots and lots of time. Not just your child's time, but *your* time, energy, and effort as well.

Excellence also requires compromise.

There's a popular ideology about creating "well-rounded children." This idea revolves around giving children a balance of this and that, and allowing them to excel in a number of areas.

It sounds like a good idea to allow children to try lots of different things like academic clubs, sports, arts, and archery club. And there should be a time and place for this. But it breeds mediocrity. If a child plays the violin, then switches to the piano, to the guitar, to the drums, to the saxophone … he's unlikely to be good at any of them.

You've heard the phrase, "Jack of all trades, master of none." Does this describe the future that we're hoping for our kids?

To become a master, we must teach our children focus. We can allow time for experimentation with multiple instruments and different activities, but eventually, to become a master, a choice should be made. It also requires the sacrifice of time, which significantly affects the activities your child can participate in.

I've said things that don't sound like a lot of fun. Words like "commitment," "practicing," and "compromise."

Ugh … who wants that?

Well, I'd argue that most people don't. There are limited amounts of musical prodigies, athletes, artists, inventors, etc. And it has nothing to do with talent (remember the previous chapter, "Is my child talented?"). The reason is that it's hard.

There's not a 5-step plan. It's more like a practice 10,000-hours plan.

And even though many people might say they want to do that, when it comes down to actually putting in the time, they won't do it.

Now, I always try to be honest (eat my vegetables and take my vitamins), even though what I say might differ from what you've heard before, or be really hard to put into practice.

#joinaband

How to raise a musical prodigy is a question I've been asked often. **The answer is always simple, but it's so hard to do.**

1 Start young.

2 Practice a lot.

3 Focus, focus, focus.

Before I finish this chapter, I want to tell you something that I wish somebody had told me as a young kid learning to play the violin.

Join a band.

For all you parents with young guitarists, drummers, and singers at home, I'm probably preaching to the choir. But I'd give the same advice to parents of violists, clarinetists, and trumpet players.

Orchestra, band, or even jazz band are the usual large group opportunities for children (remember these groups usually only start around 5th grade, and may not be available in many schools). Now, these can be great, but they can also be incredibly boring.

Have you ever wondered why there are so few tuba or French horn players? Look at the parts they get to play in band ("have" to play may be a better description). Playing the same two notes over and over again for five minutes can't be anyone's idea of a good time (and I played French horn in the band, so I know!).

So, I'm encouraging you to find a small group or band (but not the marching band...yet) for your child to join. If you want your kid to develop mastery on his or her instrument and enjoy while they're doing it, find a small group for them to join. Many community music schools offer these kind of opportunities for kids, and if there aren't any around, create your own. Start a Google group, and talk to some parents at your kid's school or local music center.

Experiment with different styles like rock, jazz, classical, hip-hop, etc. This group could become the inspiration that makes your child want to practice at home. Find small performance opportunities for the band like community events, nursing homes, or outdoor concerts (ever watch those rock band documentaries with the band managers and booking agents...that could be you).

There are no easy ways to train a gifted artist, but doing it alongside a friend is one way to keep the inspiration alive in your child's heart.

CHALLENGE #6

If your child has been playing an instrument for over 12 months, it's time to join a band! Do some research in your area, and discover what opportunities there are for children. **Write them down below with an email and phone number, and then contact them...now!**

_____

_____

_____

_____

_____

_____

_____

_____

_____

_____

_____

So, you think you can't dance?

CHAPTER SEVEN

So, you think you can't dance?

Besides the screaming, sleepless nights, and the constant search for my kids in the clothing aisles at Kohl's, being a parent is one of the most freeing attributes of my life. If you have young kids in particular, like me, then you may just be the coolest person that they've ever met. Let that sink in for a moment.

I don't know about you, but I absolutely love to dance. I do have a problem though about being a bit shy. And so, with that being said, I'm probably not the first one up on the dance floor when Maroon 5 is on the radio.

Now that I have my own kids, I want them to experience and know how amazing it is to dance (I also remember the group of girls in summer camp that lined up to dance with the one guy who had any moves...and it wasn't me). There were far too many Junior and High School dances where I stood glued to the wall like a moron because I thought I was too cool to dance, and even if I wasn't, I had no idea what to do anyway!

Nowadays, however, dance has become a default response in our household, and it's not just because I have an incredible shoulder roll. Children don't

judge, and so, whatever seemed embarrassing before, with kids, it's incredible and amazing and they want to do it right now! (There's a self-esteem boost for all you parents out there!)

One of the easiest ways to implement dance in your home is with an impromptu dance party. In our house, we have a nightly bedtime routine into which we usually weave in dance a few times a week. There's no plan. We really just turn on some music and break into improvised dance movements. We're not serious at all, and more often than not, it results in a lot of jumping and running around in circles (we recently got these super long bean bags...they seem to have a sign hidden on them somewhere that says "jump on me!"). One song is often all we do, but it's definitely one of the highlights of the day, and something everyone looks forward to (I often wonder what the neighbors think…).

For those of you looking for more of a purposeful experience, combining some simple musical concepts alongside a repetitive dance pattern is a great way for children to internalize musical and rhythmic ideas. Stomping or tiptoeing to different parts of the music can represent dynamics, alternating fast and slow footsteps internalizes speed or tempo, and going from crouching to standing tall can coordinate with high/low levels of pitch. As I've said throughout this book, you need not be a professional musician to teach your child music and introduce them to fundamental musical concepts. The best thing you can do as a parent is build consistency in the practice of those fundamentals.

Finally, for the brave ones out there, I highly recommend folk dancing. Now, this probably won't be the dance step of choice at a Justin Bieber concert, but for building creativity and improvisation, as well as gaining appreciation of diverse world cultures, it's hard to beat. The Orff and Kodaly methods have done a wonderful job of compiling lists of folk dances, especially those from Eastern Europe.

> ❝ Party like a preschooler!. ❞

YouTube also has a wealth of children's folk dance videos, so all you need to do there is party like a preschooler!

Dancing is a beautiful way to connect with your child, to discover the music and dance cultures of the world, and to experience a new kind of freedom and joy in your life. I hope this chapter takes some of your anxiety away regarding dancing and gives you some new tools to try with your child.

CHALLENGE #7

Pick a time this week to hold a dance party with your kids (planned or unplanned) and write about how it goes below.

_____

_____

_____

_____

_____

_____

_____

_____

_____

_____

_____

_____

_____

_____

_____

Why cellists
score higher
on the SAT

CHAPTER EIGHT

Why cellists
score higher
on the SAT

Yes, I've seen the headlines too. Music makes kids smarter.

They read better.

Talk better.

They add and subtract better.

**And overall, they just look better (ok ...
I made that last part up).**

We all know that. But, why exactly does music make kids smarter? Harvard says this, Northwestern University says that, who's to know?

As a parent, music can be something of a conundrum.

Do I play music to the kid when he's in the womb?

Do I buy my child a bunch of Baby Einstein toys to play with?

Do we need to go to the "Mommy and me" music class together next week?

#musiciansarecool

Let's take a trip down memory lane (fill in your own sound effects here).

Remember high school, and all those tests you didn't really study for? Yeah, don't lie to yourself, I know you didn't study for some until the night before. What do we call that again? Cramming, anyone?

So, what are we doing when we prepare for a test at the last minute?

Essentially, we're trying to stuff a lot of information into our head over a short a period of time, and this is usually reinforced by repetition.

Works every time, right?

Now, compare that to actual studying. If you thought what I just described was actual studying, then this might be new.

Alright, so let's say you have a math test every Friday. Each day you're in school learning new concepts, and so your brain is working. But where the magic really happens is in study hall … wait, no one actually studies in study hall (best waste of time...ever!), so the magic actually happens at home, when your friends aren't passing notes about who's got a crush on who. That's the time when you sit down and review what you just learned, and then you practice it. You repeat that process of reviewing and practicing it every day until the test.

What does that do other than keeping you inside your room and not bothering your parents? It strengthens your memory. And what does school emphasize in testing more than anything?

Drum roll … Memory!

What year was the Declaration of Independence signed? Hmm … let me remember.

What was the dog's name in the story you just read?

Can't remember? Then it sounds like you need some practice.

I'll bring it back to music. What's one thing that musicians do more of than probably anyone else?

They (musicians) memorize the music they're playing.

You've probably had to memorize things like famous speeches, poems, Bible verses, and grocery lists (give me the actual list, Mom!). Imagine if someone asked you to memorize, word for word, the first few chapters of a book. If you could do that, you would probably think that you were amazing. And you would be, because that's hard...but let me bring you back to earth for a moment.

Most advanced string players (including our cellist friends) are doing the equivalent of this by the time they're in their early teens (or elementary school for the great ones). My friends and I were memorizing 20-30 pages of music when we were this age (not braggin', just sayin').

> 66 You've got to exercise your brain. 99

The only way you can do it though, is through consistency and repetition (cramming won't work here). You've got to exercise your brain. And just like any other muscle, when you work it out, you make it stronger, and so it becomes easier and easier to remember things ... like all the information you'll need for the SAT or ACT.

So then, do all musicians score better on tests?

No.

However, there is a direct relationship between academic success in school and memorization, and from where I'm sitting, music is one of the best ways to do it.

CHALLENGE #8

Pick something to memorize this week and make sure it's not super easy. Maybe a passage you've highlighted from a book, or a favorite quote. Write about how you did it. Was it harder than you thought? Would you do it again? **Write down anything you did that made the process easier.**

One thing every parent
can do to raise a
musical child

CHAPTER NINE

One thing every parent
can do to raise a
musical child

Parents tell me all the time, *"Oh, I wish I still played a musical instrument like you."* I usually look at them, and ask them, *"Why are you still talking to me? Go and learn one already!"* As adults, we have this idea that we can't learn music. People say that since they didn't start young, they'll never be able to play the violin, piano, guitar, or whatever. I think it's stupid, and I think it's wrong. When you became a parent, did you think, "I wish I had done this earlier. I'll never be able to do it now."? No! Once you bring that baby home from the hospital you get to work.

I want to tell you about one thing I believe every parent can do to raise a musical child. Now, I know some of you are thinking, that sounds great, but I don't sing or play a musical instrument, or I'm tone deaf. Well, I don't care if you can't do those things, and since you're reading this right now, you're probably thinking there is some secret answer hidden somewhere. I believe you're right. But first, let me tell you what parents shouldn't do to raise a musical child.

❶ Don't make an iPad your child's music teacher

I don't hate iPads; I think they actually have great apps for children. But relying on an app itself to teach your child can be counterproductive. An unattended child with an iPad is likely to get stuck on exciting graphics or the fast pace of the program (ever seen a child on an iPad in the airport? Can you say "zombie"?). A study performed by Georgetown University showed that the keys to beneficial screen time are interactivity and adult participation. It's these things that help children learn better than passive viewing of the material.

❷ A private music teacher alone can't teach your child

My parents enrolled me in private music lessons, and I'll admit that it worked for me. However, it doesn't work for every child, and not every parent can afford to spend the money or time it requires from them.

Besides that, it's nearly useless if the parent is not practicing with the child at home.

It doesn't matter if you bring your daughter to the best cello teacher in town, if she's not getting support from Mom and Dad, or putting in practice time at home, she's not going to learn much.

③ School music programs are highly limited

Many schools don't start music classes until 4th or 5th grade, so this can be a major hurdle for parents with young children. Additionally, most school programs that do exist only take place once a week. Just like with private music lessons, if it's not happening at home too, you're probably not going to see a big benefit. So, how in the world do you raise a musical child? Well, having learned this way myself, I'll tell you.

Learn alongside your child.

What?? You might be asking yourself right now.

Learn with my kid? Yes. Learn with your kid.

Sure, there are a lot of excuses you could give:

❶ That's embarrassing.

❷ What if he/she's better than me? (So what? That'd probably be a good thing anyway, right?)

❸ I don't think I can.

Most parents want to spend more time with their kids. And a lot of the parents I talk to often wonder what they can do together with their kids when they have that time. Well, guess what you can do? Learn music together. Set aside some time to listen to music together. If you like singing, teach your kids some songs, and don't be afraid to use those iPad apps I talked about earlier, just as long as you're doing them together. Music should be a shared experience, and the best person your child can learn it from is you.

66 The keys to beneficial screen time are interactivity with adult participation. 99

CHALLENGE #9

Listen to some music or learn something musical
with your child and talk about it together.
Describe how it went below.

_____

_____

_____

_____

_____

_____

_____

_____

_____

_____

_____

_____

_____

How to expand your child's musical taste buds...

How to expand your child's musical taste buds...

Have you ever fasted or restrained from something (and I don't mean exercise)? Maybe it was food, television, video games, or social media. Remember what it felt like to experience that "thing" again? After not eating for a few days, let me tell you, a chicken sandwich tastes absolutely amazing. Not that it doesn't always taste amazing, but after that time away, it's got that extra "je ne sais quoi."

Or maybe you're a foodie and you love cooking recipes from different cookbooks. I read Daniel Meyer's autobiography (the founder of Shake Shack) in which he claims that he literally traveled the world, multiple times, solely to eat food. Sign me up!

I like to think that **our ears have taste buds.** Anatomically (what a great word!), they're called ossicles. It's the part of your body that experiences the wonder of sound.

Think about the range of emotions you feel in your body from the pulsating, driving force of Beethoven's 5th Symphony to the powerful, beautiful anthem of Bono and U2 in a "Beautiful Day" to the soul-searching devastation of Gary Jules, "Mad World." I could go on.

Anyone remember the mixtape? When you had something special to tell someone, but maybe you didn't quite have the words to do it. Cue the mixtape. When I was a high school senior (why do all my stories seem to come from high school?), a foreign exchange student from China gave me a mixtape with all kinds of Chinese music. I played it repeatedly on my tape deck, because it was so different than anything else I'd ever heard in my life.

The summer after I graduated, I went to a summer music camp in California, and I heard people playing Latin music, rock music, and even African tribal music on the violin. It stunned me. I bought their CDs and played them repeatedly. It was like an insatiable hunger inside of me craving this music, to understand and experience it.

I think there's an incredible gift we, as parents, can give to our kids. And it's something that every parent can give. If you're a professional musician or you struggle to keep a beat, it doesn't matter. And don't downplay it either. Show them

Share the music that you're passionate about with your kids.

what you think is the best song ever. Whenever "Forever Young" comes on the radio when I'm with my kids (well, honestly it doesn't really matter who I'm with …) I get excited. I sing along way louder than I probably should, and I'm always dancing. I can't help what that song does to me, and I won't apologize. My kids know what I'm passionate about, and they love getting excited about it with me. Yeah, maybe they won't want to walk down the streets singing and dancing "Mamma Mia" when they're 17, but who knows (I'm still doing it).

I think in listening to music, we can get really lazy. Again, going back to the food thing; it's easy to just make the same five recipes each week (apologies to my children for their father's lunch packing skills). But it gets more interesting when you try something new. Add something to the menu like a Hungarian Kürtoskalács (chimney cake). Your sweet tooth is calling!

If you like Rock and Roll, try listening to new artists that you've never heard before. Find a list of the top 100 Rock and Roll artists and find music from each artist (it's pretty fun), or just find the ones that you've never heard of before. Try listening to a new genre of music all together. Words like popular and familiar don't necessarily mean that something is "good" (Case study: McDonald's). Sample the music of an Indonesian gamelan orchestra, Mongolian throat singers, or a Swedish nyckelharpa. Spotify is a great platform to find all these diverse types of music and to DJ your car ride home each day.

Personally, I love exposing my kids to the music of different countries. Our family travels a lot around the United States and internationally, and I enjoy hearing the music from different places. I remember while we were all in Kazakhstan, on the spur of the moment, we went to a folk music concert, and I literally had my mouth on the floor watching and listening to the traditional dances and music.

> **"Music is a communal activity. Do it together."**

While we're at home, I curate or prepare a lot of cultural content for my kids to listen to. Right now, we're studying France, and we're learning a bunch of French folk songs together. It's fun, it's educational, and it's a connecting point you can make, if you want, every day with your kids. And in so many ways, that's what it comes down to. Music is a communal activity. Do it together, bring your kids in, explore, and have fun.

CHALLENGE #10

Find a musical artist, culture, or genre that you know little to nothing about and sit with your kids to listen to it. Then talk about it together. Did you like it, hate it, not really care? What was unique about it? And most important … what can you explore next! **Write all about it.**

_____

_____

_____

_____

_____

_____

_____

_____

_____

_____

_____

_____

_____

_____

Why you shouldn't sing in the shower

CHAPTER ELEVEN

Why you shouldn't
sing in the shower

You've seen the movie, *Elf*, before, right? The one with Will Ferrell? As much as I enjoy the movie, my wife's insistence on watching it every year is slightly lessening its charm.

Remember the scene after Buddy has just met Jovie, the female elf from the department store, and he's listening to her while she's singing in the shower? After a while, Buddy can't help himself, and he joins her in song. At that point, Jovie realizes she's not alone, screams at her unwanted chorus member, and Buddy makes a quick exit from the women's room.

Later in the movie, Buddy shares with his friend, one of the great mottos of the North Pole "The best way to spread Christmas Cheer is singing loud for all to hear."

I love this. Buddy may not really be an elf, but he's totally on to something.

This past Christmas my family and I actually met Buddy the elf at the public library (it was amazing, just so you know). I love to sing at the top of my lungs … and sometimes, even in public, so we've become fast friends.

Biologically, singing releases endorphins in your brain, which make you feel good. And when you take deep breaths while singing, it draws more oxygen into your blood, creating better circulation.

> **"Singing is meant to be shared."**

If you've ever been around a preschool music class, singing is one of the best parts of the day; it produces a domino effect in a group.

Let's go back to our elf, Buddy, again. At the end of the movie, his girlfriend starts singing a Christmas carol in a group of confused New Yorkers. His mother-in-law joins in, then her son, and others, until everyone is singing. It's contagious.

And that's why you shouldn't sing in the shower! Singing is meant to be shared. Sing in your living room, where everyone can hear you and join in. If you don't like the sound of your voice, or feel embarrassed to sing, then be silly about it. My dad has never been a crooner, but every time a birthday comes around, he makes an effort, and he's silly about it, which makes it fun for everybody.

Now, I'm not hating on the bathroom shower divas out there, but it's a bummer if that's the only place where you feel comfortable enough to sing. Kids love to sing, and they love to be a part of something. And if you're concerned your kids will make fun of you, don't be. Opening yourself up and engaging with your child through song is unlikely to receive a vocal critique from an 8-year-old.

So, grab a songbook, sing along to some recordings, or plan a living room karaoke night together. If you're a gamer, then Rock Band for the Xbox or PlayStation is an obvious choice. I've had some of my absolute favorite moments playing Rock Band with kids and adults.

So, get out of the shower, and make some noise.

CHALLENGE #11

Plan a singing night in your house using one of
the suggestions I've mentioned above (or if you
have an idea for something completely different, go
for it). **Write about how it went.**

_____

_____

_____

_____

_____

_____

_____

_____

_____

_____

_____

_____

_____

Why your child shouldn't listen to classical music

Why your child shouldn't listen to classical music

Alright, so this chapter's topic probably has you scratching your head. You thought that classical music was the be all, end all for promoting intelligence in kids?

Right?

Then, why do so few parents actually play classical music for their kids?

How often do you put on a recording of a Bach chorale, Wagner Opera, or Haydn Symphony for your 3-year-old?

Probably not often, I'm guessing …

But is it actually good for child development? … Most definitely, it is!

Classical repertoire, as we know it, owns the market when it comes to intellectual music (some jazz aficionados may dispute this). If you've ever listened to a Schoenberg Symphony or a Webern Opera, you'll know these pieces are meant to provoke your thought process as much as they are to stimulate your enjoyment.

The reason classical music is so good for children, is that it stimulates the brain. Sophisticated rhythms, melodies, and harmonies intertwine to create a mixture of sounds for a child's mind to explore. Classical music is meant to be engaged with, to be talked about.

Last year, I visited a variety of art museums in Paris with my family. At first, it was rather boring for the kids (who were 3 and 5 at the time). We saw paintings of mountains, lakes, picnics, and naked people (well, that was a conversation starter!), but nothing really caught their attention. So, I tried to be more intentional about it.

"Hey, did you see that guy hiding in the corner of that painting? What was he holding in his hand?"

Or. "How did that painting make you feel when you looked at it?"

And "If you were painting a picture of a bridge, how would

you paint it?"

Now, I won't lie and say they were instantly transformed, with art suddenly coming alive to them for the first time. But I can say that they became interested, and actually stopped begging to leave and get ice cream cones.

Music and art deserve to be pondered and discussed. Much of the

world of classical music remains a mystery because time and attention haven't been devoted to understanding it. And that's what leads to much of the disinterest in classical music, or even jazz and folk music. It's fun and interesting at first, but then if we're unable to deepen our understanding, it eventually becomes frustrating and dull.

If you've ever tried to learn a musical instrument on your own, it's likely that you've experienced this in some way. And it's probably why people still pay to take music lessons with a real person, rather than just watching the untold thousands of free tutorials online. We want understanding, and often it's not enough to look for it on a screen.

I know it sounds strange to say this, but kids shouldn't listen to classical music without preparation. Sure, some kids will love it, and if they do, then cultivate it. But really, most won't. The real loss here is that they'll choose not to listen to it in the future, because they had no idea what they were listening to when they heard it the first time.

Now, you need not be a professor in music history to help your kids out here. When you listen to something, ask them questions about what they hear. How do they respond to the music? With classical music in particular, it's helpful to have special times to just listen to the music … not talk, but to sit silently and experience the music. There's a reason museums are quiet. They want to allow the spectator to concentrate, and similarly, to get the most out of classical music your child needs to focus.

I'm a big fan of learning things along with your kids (can you tell?). So, to create a deeper experience here, try listening to something with your kids, and then get online to look up the composer and read what other people think about the piece. You can even try listening to different versions of the same piece. Hearing several artists perform classical repertoire is like listening to a group of really good cover bands. No one knows exactly what the composer really meant, but they're all treating the music differently to make it their own.

So, be intentional about listening to music with your kids. There's a lot of music that's much easier to digest, and requires little to any thought, but there's room for a challenge sometimes. I'm not opposed to pop music, but listening to the Top 40 isn't likely to provide a whole lot of brain stimulation.

Try mixing it up. It doesn't have to be every day, but by introducing your children to the world of classical music, you're not only doing something that's healthy for their brain, but you're opening new possibilities of enjoyment for a lifetime to come.

CHALLENGE #12

Throw a listening party!
Select a piece of classical repertoire, and sit down
as a family to listen to it in silence, and then talk
about it. **Write about which pieces you listened
to and what your family thought about them.**

_____

_____

_____

_____

_____

_____

_____

_____

_____

_____

_____

_____

How to nurture a love of music
in your child

How to nurture a love of music *in your child*

Americans love to have fun. Theme parks, arcades, and casinos dot the landscape. I recently joined a new gym, and the exercise bicycles not only have a television screen, but also include games that allow you to bike through the Swiss Alps and other gorgeous landscapes. As I was swimming laps the other day, I thought to myself how boring it was, and how much better it would be if I could listen to an audiobook … underwater.

Now, I'm not here to rail against technology or demean it, as I enjoy watching Netflix on my 4K TV as much as the next person. But I think that the evolving idea of what is fun, and the importance of "fun" in our lives has distorted perceptions.

Let's take love and marriage. Existing thought states that love should be fun, and in certain cases that leads to marriage. However, as most married couples will admit, while it's fun at times, marriage is hard, sometimes upsetting, and requires a lot of work.

I've heard a lot of parents say they want their children to "love" music. Now, I like to be a bit controversial, so I'll take a stab at clarifying the difference between a "love" of music and an "acquaintance" with it.

Love is based on relationships. If I told you I was a Green Bay Packers fan and that I watched every game, knew the player stat sheets, and had made a pilgrimage to Lambeau field, you would believe that I had what could be described as a "relationship" with the team. If I said that I "loved" the Packers, you probably wouldn't think it to be an unusual thing to say (although you might think that a one-sided relationship like that is unhealthy … but that's another conversation, and a separate visit to the therapist).

If someone else came along who saw that the Packers were favored to win the Super Bowl this year (and it seems they are most years), and said that he "loved" the team, but hadn't really paid any attention to them before, you'd probably pick that person out as a fake, or someone just "jumping on the bandwagon".

You can't have a relationship with someone or something that you don't spend significant time with or invest in.

Many parents are looking for quick and easy ways to create "well rounded children." The extra curriculars pile up, often resulting in a child who has been exposed to many disciplines but can't do any of them well. And music, is a jealous lover.

If any of you have seen the 1998 film, the Red Violin, you may remember a scene in which the main character (a young boy), sleeps with his violin. As we see the child grow and age, we witness an inseparable bond with the instrument. We see a love affair develop between the man and the instrument, resulting in the beautiful music we hear throughout the film.

Recently, I interviewed Donnell Leahy and Natalie MacMaster, two world renowned fiddlers, who now spend much of their time performing with their young children. An assumed part of their children's daily routine is to spend time with their violins. Now what really surprised me, was that they told me this time isn't necessarily spent practicing the instrument. It might be as simple as holding onto the instrument during a television show, or while sitting in the living room reading a book.

It struck me as an action of someone intentionally pursuing a relationship with music. Donnell and Natalie both told me they have no intention to pressure their children into life as professional musicians, but their goal is to raise them in a home where they are actively learning how to love music. They, themselves, grew up in a disappearing culture where music was simply everywhere, from the street corner to the fisherman's wharf, to the pub. However, as that culture fades, they still feel the importance of giving their children an understanding of what that love can look like.

> "Building a relationship with music is hard."

As parents, we sometimes confuse "what's best" with "how much"; but more doesn't always equal better.

Much of the teaching around music is about how to make it "fun and easy," so kids can enjoy a lifetime of music. Unfortunately, as I have noticed throughout my career, this rarely works. I've had hundreds of people come after performances and tell me how they wish they would have kept up the violin, the piano, or whatever instrument they had played.

Leopold Mozart, the unsung hero and father of young

Amadeus, was a composer, violinist, and music teacher. Responsible for much of the younger Mozart's early musical training, Leopold, Amadeus, and his sister, Nanneri, actively performed together in concert tours throughout Europe. Now that's doing music together!

Building a relationship with music is hard, and it takes time and patience. I also want to point out that it doesn't require proficiency in an instrument. There are plenty of individuals with a fine understanding and appreciation of the art form, who cannot play an instrument, and who could easily be said to be lovers of music (you don't need to be a football player to be a Monday morning quarterback).

So, in a moment of encouragement, I urge you parents (if you're still reading, I assume that's you!) to ignite a love of music in your child by intentionally walking the journey with them.

CHALLENGE #13

Write about what a love of music looks like
in your family now, or what you imagine it could be.

_____

_____

_____

_____

_____

_____

_____

_____

_____

_____

_____

_____

_____

Skip the bill,

do music at home

Skip the bill,
do music at home

Having kids is expensive (at least that's what the marketing companies out there tell us).

When I had my first kid, I didn't worry much about the cost. She was breastfed, we were gifted a pack 'n play and a stroller, and she slept in our room. Besides diapers (thank you Amazon!), we barely spent anything on her (our friends donated most of her clothes and toys).

When my second child was born, his pediatrician told us he needed hypoallergenic formula, which costs over $35 a can, and which only lasted a few days. My expectations for the cost of having children grew substantially after that appointment.

However, it's only been most recently (now with four kids) that I've seen the tremendous price tag that comes with school tuition, having a home that can accommodate six people (a two-bedroom home only works for so long with four kids), food costs (now that everyone is eating real food, and lots of it), and extra curriculars.

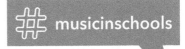

I took my family to a corn maze a few weeks ago. I'm used to paying about $10-15 for the adults, and the kids getting in for free or for a few dollars. This time, I spent over a hundred dollars to get into the maze along with a few cold cider donuts.

Now, we've just started going through adding extra curriculars and sports (so, my hat is off to you parents in the thick of it). Swimming lessons, dance class, gymnastics, and so on. It's manageable for one or two kids, but when you're seeing hundreds of dollars debited from your account for swim lessons each month, and you're not sure if your kids like to swim (or if they'll even get in the pool)… it's terrifying!

Unfortunately, music is often lacking in daycares and schools, or it's so infrequent that kids can't remember what they learned since the last time they saw their teacher. To pick up the slack, Mommy and Me classes make up the difference, with locations all around the world through programs like Music Together or Gymboree. Again, $12-15 per class doesn't seem like a big deal, until you have two, three, or more kids in each session, and then you're paying out hundreds of dollars to sing Old MacDonald had a cash register.

Now, Mommy and Me programs can be great, and they're providing a service that many people want. But, as engaging as some early childhood music teachers can be, it can't compare to a mom or dad doing music at home with their child, which is not as hard as you think.

I do music at home with my kids every night. It's a ritual that we have. After dinner, we get together in the living room and we sing. It's not very complicated. We use an illustrated cultural songbook from Fiddlefox (right now, we're doing France), and we read and sing along in the native language, followed by the English translation. When we're first learning, we use an accompanying recording, but after we've sung it a few times, we try to sing without it. By the way, my kids are 6, 4, 2 and 2. So, we're not overcomplicating things. Sometimes a child runs off in the middle of a song, comes back to hit someone who then starts screaming, and eventually sits down with the rest of us (that's what happened last night at least). I try not to stop too much and correct or scold the kids during the process. I encourage all of my kids to participate, but sometimes they just don't want to do it, and it's fine (if you want to pick your nose and sit in the corner, by all means, do it).

When my second child was three years old, he would constantly surprise me with the way that he learned music. He would rarely be part of the music session, and seemed as though he wasn't paying attention, but the next day, he'd be singing the songs word for word.

Simplicity and routine are some of our core values as a family. We learn about four new songs every two months. That way it's easy for the kids to learn them by heart, and even sing them in a foreign language. We also teach the children sign language or a simple movement routine to accompany each song.

It's also important to do it frequently. We plan to sing together every night, but sometimes it doesn't happen, and that's okay. It's an intentional part of each day (which only takes 6-8 minutes), and we plan our days and nighttime routine to include that.

> 66 Music brings richness to family life. 99

You can also increase the level of difficulty and vary the content. Before we had our 2-year-old twins joining the sessions, we would create our own dances or find cultural folk dances to connect with the music. It's also fun to change the speed of the song (great for songs about planes and trains!), or alter how loud or soft you can be while singing. Percussive sounds like clapping hands, stomping feet, snapping, or patting your knees are easy for anyone to add into a song, and are core rhythmic activities of the Orff Method.

Music brings richness to family life, and can be a beautiful way for parents to connect with their children daily. It can be difficult to find a way to connect with your children on a regular basis, and the simple act of singing with your kids can become a bonding experience they will remember for their lifetime.

CHALLENGE #14

Pick a song or a songbook to sing with your kids.
Write about the song that you picked and what the
experience was like for your family.
Was it harder or easier than you thought?

_____

_____

_____

_____

_____

_____

_____

_____

_____

_____

_____

_____

_____

How old should I be *before my child starts* playing an instrument?

How old should I be *before my child starts* playing an instrument?

In 10 years of teaching music, one of the most commonly asked questions I've heard from parents has to be, "how old should my children be before they start learning an instrument?"

If you have kids playing an instrument, you've probably asked it too.

But, I think it's the wrong question.

You could ask how old kids usually are when they start playing an instrument, but I'd advise you not to. Instead, as the parent, ask yourself how old would you like to be before your child starts playing an instrument? All four of my children started playing a musical instrument at age 2, and I wish I had started them earlier.

And no, I didn't just misspeak, and say something crazy. I really believe that learning an instrument depends a whole lot more on you than it does your child.

Who will get them an instrument?

Who will drive them to lessons?

Who will practice with them?

Who will buy them their books?

Who will hug and reassure them when they cry and say they can't do it?

Learning music is a commitment, one which I think every parent can partner with their child to achieve. But I advise moms and dads to have their eyes wide open during the ordeal. If you can't practice with your kid, don't bother. You're wasting your money and you're better off spending your time and money on something else.

But, if you can commit, then the age question becomes more for you than for your child.

I started all my kids on instruments at age 2.

Was it frustrating?

Yes.

Was it fun?

Not really.

Was it helpful?

Absolutely.

Would I do it again?

I'd do it with every child.

Now, there are some physical limitations for young children. Wind instruments aren't appropriate for small kids since they haven't developed enough control in their breathing yet. Instruments like the violin and piano are the most common for young children, as are drums, percussion, and other mallet-based instruments, such as the Orff instruments. Desk bells are another accessible option. I've also experimented with miniature guitars or ukuleles, which work pretty well.

You can note that I don't mention singing, as developing the voice should be encouraged to happen alongside the learning of any instrument.

So, for you non-believers out there, let's actually talk about what you do with a 2-year-old violinist.

Learn where to put your feet (walk before you run ... right?)

Learn how to care for the instrument, how to pick it up, and how to put it away

(You'd be amazed how many kid don't intuitively know how to close a case before picking it up again. Cause and effect... there's some physics for you).

Learn how to hold the violin in playing position and in rest position.

Learn how to put the bow on the string.

And guess what? ... That's the first couple of years (not a typo).

You don't even need an instrument for the first year ... a Kleenex box, stirring stick, and a wooden dowel will get you that far.

It's not even about music initially.

It's discipline.

It's motor control.

It's consistency.

It's relationship.

It's concentration.

How Old Should I Be Before My Child Starts Playing an Instrument? **119**

Italian educator Maria Montessori and founder of the Montessori method said "Concentration is the key that opens up to the child the latent treasures within him."

At this tender age, we're opening up the child to the beautiful experience of music. What an incredible opportunity to join him or her in this journey.

66 Concentration is the key that opens up to the child the latent treasures within him. 99

CHALLENGE #15

Have you ever played an instrument? If so, how old were you when you started? **Write about your experience (the good, bad, and the ugly) in the section below.**

_____

_____

_____

_____

_____

_____

_____

_____

_____

_____

_____

_____

_____

_____

But ...
I'm not good with kids

CHAPTER SIXTEEN

But ...
I'm not good with kids

Sometimes I think we all need a good kick in the pants.
And if this next part applies to you, then consider yourself
"kicked".

I hear people using the excuse they aren't good with kids to
justify not doing certain things with their children. Now, if
you feel uncomfortable with children or you simply don't
like kids, then yes, stay out of the education business. But if
you're a parent, dude, man up (and for womenfolk out there,
which this seems less of a problem for anyway, woman up)!

Now, I know I'm throwing all kinds of crazy at you here,
and I realize that some of it will stick, and some of it won't.
But the biggest non-starter is this whole "I'm not good with
kids" thing. If that's your shtick, then drop that line like a hot

potato (fun game BTW), and get yourself in a

room with some kids.

I get that past experiences and relationships can bring difficulty to the parental role. Maybe your dad wasn't around, your mom was always yelling, or you got bullied in school. When you become a parent yourself, however, you enter into one of the most sacred and important relationships you will ever have in your life.

I'm not here to write a manifesto on parenting or give you a 7- step plan on being the best parent you can be. If you're looking for some straight up parenting advice, check out anything by Dr. James Dobson. I do, however, strongly believe in two core concepts.

❶ Intentionally spend time with your kids... every day.

❷ Speak affirmation over your kids (yes... you should do this every day too).

So, the first thing. Spend time with your kids. Uhh ... that's kind of obvious, right? So why don't more people do it?

Years ago, I met a set of parents with a nanny. The nanny would pick up their kids in the morning from their house and bring them to daycare at 7:30 a.m. Then at 6 p.m., the nanny would pick the children up from daycare, bring them home, cook them dinner, and put them to bed.

When I heard that, I was in shock … How could the parents possibly have time to spend with their kids? The answer they gave me stunned me.

Mom and Dad would wake up every day at 4 a.m. to spend several uninterrupted hours with both of their children before going to work each day. Even though they had demanding jobs that required them to work from early in the morning to late at night, they found a way to intentionally spend time with their kids.

Being a parent requires sacrifice. For parents of a newborn, it's not so much of a choice, as it is a requirement to survive those first years. You can't go through life the same way anymore. Every child requires intentional time and attention to feel valued, to be known, to be part of a loving relationship with Mom or Dad. It may not require you to take up the graveyard shift at 4 a.m., but it will require something.

Being together can be simple. I was reading a book yesterday afternoon on my bean bag couch (yes, they are awesome!), and my four-year-old son came up to me and said he really wanted to sit with me and read his book next to me while I read mine. So we read together for an hour. No words spoken

… just sitting together on a purple bean bag.

Boys are strong, and girls are beautiful. That's how I approach my children, although my daughter could probably pummel any of her brothers, and my youngest son has the most beautiful and angelic face I've ever seen. Kids need to know they're valued, and they'll know this by what you say to them, repeatedly.

Three years ago, I began a ritual of speaking words of affirmation over my children every night. There was some variety in it, and while the words differed for each child, I came back to similar themes each night. We rarely talked about it any other time during the day.

> **" Parenting isn't meant for professionals. "**

One day, after doing this for several months, I asked my son who he was, and he started speaking back to me all the words that I had spoken about him that year.

There is power in the words that you speak. King Solomon wrote in the book of Proverbs that "your words are so powerful that they will kill or give life."

Make it life you speak over your children, your spouse, your friends, everyone in your path.

Parenting isn't meant for professionals, but it's the parents who teach the professionals what life can be.

CHALLENGE #16

Write down your experience in encouraging your kids at home and building them up as people. **What habits or routines do you use to make it a regular part of your lives?**

_____

_____

_____

_____

_____

_____

_____

_____

_____

_____

_____

_____

CHAPTER SEVENTEEN

When can we quit?

CHAPTER SEVENTEEN

When can we quit?

I rarely meet people who hate music. And I don't think I've ever had anyone complain that they learned too much about music as a kid. Though I have heard people talk about how useless most of those advanced high school math classes were.

Maybe you didn't like some of your teachers in school and because of that you now hate science (personally, my art and crafts teachers sucked, and so when I try to draw a picture of an animal for my kids, they'd get a better drawing from the local kindergarten). Maybe you had a textbook that smelled like a toilet and it made American History a disgrace. Who knows? So much of who we are is defined by our experiences.

As a child, I hated eating fish, because we couldn't buy it fresh. We always bought it frozen, and it felt like I was eating a steak … but it wasn't, and it tasted kind of fishy. When I moved to Boston and had fresh fish, I couldn't believe it was the same animal.

Now most parents would agree that a healthy dose of music is good for their kid. Right?

But what if your kid hates it? What if he refuses to practice, whines and cries, or purposefully misplaces his books?

Is there a time to call it quits?

Music has been a part of the entirety of human history.

It's a defining feature of our humanity. We sleep, work, and eat, but we live to experience beauty, and one of the most powerful ways we do so is through music.

Confucius said, "Music produces a kind of pleasure which human nature cannot do without."

If there is such a proclivity in our nature that points towards music, and the delight in it, would we not be, as parents, doing our children a disservice by not pointing them wholeheartedly towards such joys?

Our Western education system tests children to determine competency in fields of academics determined by private parties to best prepare them for successful integration and contribution to society. I would posit that the absence of music and the arts in these lists of competencies leaves out the greatness and the goodness to what our children can be.

However, that's all a lot of philosophical yarn to unravel. Practically, when is it fair to let your kid quit music class, stop lessons, or leave the band?

While not a music educator herself, Italian scientist and master educator, Maria Montessori said "success [in music education] is bound up with the need for the production of plenty of music around the child, so that there is set up an environment calculated to develop musical sense and intelligence."

If you should know anything about Montessori, you know that she was all about the child's prepared environment.

As parents, success and longevity in music for our children relies upon the environment that we help curate at home.

My daughter took violin lessons and classes from age 3 to 5 before asking to quit. I'm a violinist, so it was only natural for me to introduce her to my native instrument and expect her to excel in it. Maybe it was that I had too lofty of expectations

or challenging practice routine

a lack of patience

not enough encouragement

or, maybe she just didn't like the violin ... and it's okay

Maybe we'll never know some of these things, especially with younger children, who can't completely articulate their feelings (not that all adults can do this either!).

I let my daughter take half a year off. While she wasn't playing the violin, we sang a lot together. We read through songbooks. We listened to a lot of music. And she started talking about playing the piano.

I bought her an upright piano a while back and started her on lessons and a practice routine. She still complains about the practice, but she faithfully does it every day, and most days she practices on her own (which is a huge win for both of us). Will she still enjoy it in two years? Maybe ... maybe not. Can I evolve a musical environment or set of expectations to fit what my child is telling me? Yes, I can.

There is the difficult question of the financial investment, however. Especially when many years and dollars have gone into learning an instrument (or maybe Mom and Dad, you've spent thousands ... or tens of thousands of dollars on an instrument). It's better to have these discussions with your child before making a huge investment.

Should a beginner cellist be playing on a ten thousand dollar instrument? "No!" Sure, they might just break it, since they don't know how to use it, but without a commitment level that comes from experience, it's a risky investment for a parent to take, not knowing if the child even wants to play the cello.

If a child has put in significant time and effort, and is showing strong signs of wanting to continue, then, a conversation is appropriate to discuss their ongoing commitment, especially knowing that Mom and Dad may be able to help purchase a better instrument.

Let me encourage you parents who might be going through this now. It's okay for a child or even a teenager to switch instruments, and experiment. The musical language of one instrument isn't lost during the transfer to another. Muscle memory is not the same between a trumpet and a clarinet, but the skills of musicianship are transferable.

In cases of frustration, you might even find children return to their original instrument, they simply needed time away.

CHALLENGE #17

Imagine that you had spent thousands of dollars on flute lessons for you child, and then one day she quit. **Write about what you would do and why.**

When is it
good enough?

When is it *good enough?*

"Good is the enemy of great. And that is one of the key reasons why we have so little that becomes great. We don't have great schools, principally because we have good schools. We don't have great government, principally because we have good government. Few people attain great lives, in large part because it is just so easy to settle for a good life." Jim Collins

"Play the music without making mistakes," my university professor said (I should clarify here...this was a demand, not a suggestion). I looked at the brand-new piece of music in front of me and thought he was an idiot. My plan until then had been to do away with any illusion of getting it right, but to hope that with a can-do attitude, I could play it well enough to get to the end.

I was wrong...he was right.

And here's why.

Generally, it's looked down upon to be a perfectionist. You don't really need to get all the answers correct… right? Perfectionism is almost looked at like a sickness or a disorder. But is it really? Or are we just settling with things being good, and not great?

I get it. There's a certain degree of survival with parenting. I've homeschooled four kids at the same time, while working a full-time job. Some days you just want to make it. And that's all. And I'm totally okay with that. Parenting is freaking hard, and tiring, and sometimes it's disheartening and disappointing. I'm not trying to depress anyone here, parenting is wonderful, but it's tough.

Back to the professor for a minute.

After I hacked and slashed my way through yet another unfortunate piece of music, my teacher stopped me and asked me why I couldn't play it perfectly. Since I'd never seen the piece before so I thought that was a silly question (but just nodded my head politely). But why didn't I play it slower, he asked me. Why couldn't I play it slow enough that I was not just likely, but extremely likely to play it correctly.

I think there's tons of life advice right there.

> **"Are we just settling with things being good, and not great?"**

With family and parenting, slower is usually better. When I was taking my Montessori teacher training, there was a particular lesson that stuck with me. I remember the instructor talking about how we must move, teach, and interact slowly with young children. But it was what she said afterwards that really got me thinking. When you do something slowly, think about how you can do it slower.

Now, I don't want to make anyone late for dance class or for morning drop off at school, but think about how much better the day could be, if you prepared enough in advance that you could do everything slower. Imagine taking your sweet time while buckling up your kids in their car seats, cooking a meal, reading a book, or enjoying breakfast together as a family in the morning. Yeah, maybe some of that stuff sounds too idyllic, but maybe not. Just don't look to me as an example. I'm not there yet!

My daughter has been practicing this piece called "The Zoo" on the piano for the last few weeks. I've been experimenting with different practice routines and decided to let her practice on her own first, and then join her towards the end.

Every day she plays this piece repeatedly, even after she's got it perfect. And what always surprises me, is that she loves doing that. Maybe it should have been more obvious to me, but I feel like I'm just now realizing that kids love to succeed. And why not, right? We like to do things well, and see that our efforts have paid off and produced something beautiful, and kids do too.

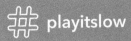

Incremental improvements or small successes as I like to call them, are what build greatness. An amazing musical performance doesn't just happen by accident, but one that results from an artist getting intimately familiar with the music.

Author Rob Bell has this to say about studying literature, and I think it describes music, absolutely wonderfully (I also feel that two adjectives in a row is simply a lot of fun). I'll insert the "music" instead of the words "sacred text." Here it is.

"[music] is like a jewel. It's like a precious stone and when you turn it the light refracts in different ways... So we're exploring. It was never like there is a finite endpoint, if you just get there then you're right. It's always about the hunt, the struggle, the doubt, the sweat, the stretching."

Wow!

Maybe I'm crazy, but I love that. The language is incredible. It's inspiring and makes me want to dig for something deeper in music and in life.

Imagine if that was the kind of excellence we taught our children to experience. What if we played music that way, or even thought about life like this?

Now, let me give you some examples of real language you can use to make and mold the music. These aren't technical terms as they are meant to communicate grandiose ideas instead of instrumental technique. Forgive my attempt to be poetic here.

"Allow the music to tell a story that captures that anguish of two characters in love that have been torn apart."

"Imagine that the song begins in the few brief moments when the sunlight breaks into the sky."

"Show me an ending that makes me feel like I've been punched in the face (don't hit me though!)."

Years ago, I had an opportunity to do a recording session with John Mayer (he's taller than I expected). During the session he didn't use a single technical term to describe what he wanted me to do on the violin (which made me wonder if he knew anything about string instruments). But it didn't matter. The way he described music was like a story. And that's what the greatest music does.

Excellence is contagious. It's exciting and it draws us to want more because we've caught the story. And that's what our children want to hold on to. They don't want to learn so they become a more well-balanced child (I feel like there's a joke swimming around here somewhere). They want to be a part of something incredible and beautiful.

CHALLENGE #18

Make up a story around a piece of music that
your child is playing (don't worry if it seems cheesy
or terrible...if you practice doing it, you'll get better too!).
Write about the story below.

15 minutes
could save you
15 dollars or more…

15 minutes
could save you
15 dollars or more…

Parents bear the weight of guilt when it comes to the lack of practice time. I can't count the apologies, excuses, and even tears (come on people!) that I witnessed while teaching private music lessons.

Is 15 minutes a day enough?

Is it ok to skip practice on weekends?

Do I need to make them practice during the summer?

Should we practice while we're on vacation?

Does my child need to wash behind his ears? (I just threw that in to see if you were paying attention)

Parents get this idea that the practice of studying music is different than any other discipline. It's not. Substitute any other subject into the equation here.

Most American schools spend the majority of the first 1-2 months of the school year teaching the class everything that they forgot during the summertime. Correct me if I'm wrong, but that seems rather inefficient.

I love Marvel comics, movies, and shows, so I will go there for a minute. As Harlem's Hero, Luke Cage, put it, "Always forward." But, how can we do that if we're spending half our time trying to remember the stuff we forgot?

Consistency is the key to any kind of study,

be it music or language, math or physics. Time invested plays a factor. There's a reason the kids in China and Japan are outperforming most of the world. Simply put, they spend more time at school. A 25% longer school year can't be nothing, right?

In my book (which you're reading), physiological predisposition + practice = talent.

Is it a generalization?

Yes.

Are there exceptions?

> "physiological predisposition + practice = talent."

Probably. When I met 10-year-old Jackie Evancho, she told me she only started singing a few months before she won America's Got Talent. Either she's a liar, or that's a whole bunch of crazy going on that I truly don't understand. (if you've never heard her sing, do it...and do it now)

So what do you do about practice time at home?

Well, first you need to determine your child's goals (or for the tiger moms out there...what your goals are).

If you want a top performer, then she's got to practice, and she's got to practice a lot. I'm not big into giving numbers, but it's multiple hours a day.

Most parents let their child take a more active role in planning. Now, I haven't met a child yet that is keen on practicing every day, but that doesn't mean parents are off the hook.

As much as Western education has devalued music and arts education, it remains a life skill that all children and adults should possess. No, we don't need a virtuoso on every street corner, but our children should be equally familiar with a 12-bar blues as they are of Pythagoras' famous theorem. And that requires time in and out of school.

So (answer the question already!), how long should my child practice every day? Enough to succeed (really...you're going to lead with that?).

Maybe 15 minutes gets it done, or maybe an hour isn't enough. Maybe your goals or a teacher's requirements need to be adjusted to come in alignment with what you feel your child can realistically achieve. Children thrive off of small successes.

My daughter just rode a bike without training wheels. She was in disbelief the first time she did it. What did she want from me? To watch her ride a bike without training wheels.

Children don't need excessive praise in response to their accomplishments (that's not to say they don't need encouragement though). They didn't do it for you anyway. Intrinsic motivation drives children (and really, anyone) to accomplish something because they can, or because it's interesting.

When a child's goals are set precisely at the edge of their grasp, that's when we see their greatest delights. If you've ever heard a child say "I didn't think I could do it, but..." you know they've achieved something that they thought was beyond belief. And most often, it drives them to want to do more, or try something even more difficult.

And that's where the role of the parent and teacher comes into play. We are assistants or guides to the child. We stretch them by helping them set objectives based on what we've observed will challenge them to succeed.

The writer and apostle, St. Paul, said this of God, "That he will not let you be tempted beyond what you can bear." It is this same calling we carry for the children in our care; that we would not let them be challenged beyond what they can handle. What good is a puzzle to an infant, or a ceiling mobile to a 5th grader (although I can imagine a classroom of elementary school kids going bananas with a room full of mobiles)?

Challenge your kids, but don't drive them to despair (you could drive them out for ice cream though!). If your child's practice ritual works, then don't change it. If they don't feel like they're doing well, then either there's too much work involved and it's too hard, or they just need more practice time. Observe and adjust.

Practicing is a moving target, it's different for everyone, and it's not the same from year to year. So, don't be afraid to experiment, or even let your kids come up with suggestions they think might work better.

Music is a team sport. So play it as one (that should absolutely be a song).

CHALLENGE #19

How much does your child practice each day?
**Describe his/her daily routine and any challenges
you're facing together.**

_____

_____

_____

_____

_____

_____

_____

_____

_____

_____

_____

_____

_____

_____

The great experiment

CHAPTER TWENTY

The great experiment

If you've never read or listened to anything by Tim Ferriss, stop reading this book now, and go check him out (don't worry, you're just about done anyway). Tim is a self-experimentor (Microsoft Word is totally hating on this word and telling me it's not real...I'll use it anyway), and has written pages and pages on the incredible ways that he's experimented to increase his health, wealth, and wisdom.

The book you're reading isn't a list of ideas. It's a collection of experiments that I've either tried at home with my own kids or in the classroom with the thousands of children I've worked with during my career.

Children need consistency in order for learning to happen. It's not instantaneous. But learning isn't static either. It evolves. And what works for one year, may not work the next.

Maria Montessori said that *"...we discovered that education is not something which the teacher does, but that it is a natural process which develops spontaneously in the human being. It is not acquired by listening to words, but in virtue of experiences in which the child acts on his environment. The teacher's task is not to talk, but to prepare and arrange a series of motives for cultural activity in a special environment made for the child."*

Did you catch that (yes, I agree, she writes in long sentences)? Education comes about spontaneously through the experiences of the child in his or her environment.

You, me, and your kids' teachers (if they're in school) need not be in the education business (although I suppose that's a conflict of interest if the department of education is writing your payroll checks). We're lab assistants to the great experiment that is your child.

Have you ever observed a classroom of infants or toddlers and looked at the artwork (if not, then Google it)? Most of the time it's really good. Straight lines, round circles, balanced presentation. One problem though...usually the kids had little or nothing to do with it. And that begs the question of why?

It's hard to be around something that sucks (and I'm not referring to a vacuum). When we encounter something that's not good, our first reaction is usually to ignore it or try to fix it.

A few months ago, I saw a bunch of posters for a free symphony orchestra concert in the next town. In my experience, that's rare to find. So, I gathered up my whole family, plus grandparents, and we took two carloads of people down to the concert. Ten seconds into the performance, I realized this had been a mistake. The orchestra was absolutely no good. Luckily, it was late, and I justified our early exit with the "kids need to get to bed" excuse.

Now, back to those art projects...

Bad art is good. In fact, it's great. If you don't believe me, check out the sell price on the painting "Interchange" by Willem de Kooning. And in those infant and toddler classrooms, bad art probably means that the kids are doing the work themselves (unless their teacher has suspect skills). And that's how they learn.

"Education," as described by Orff pedagogist, Doug Goodkin *"is concerned with wholeness, and with bringing forth that which lies within, growing from the interest and temperament of each individual and calling on his or her contribution to the process. Authentic education requires the teacher to notice and attend to the unique needs and gifts of each student. By contrast, training moves from the outside in, bringing the student through an existing body of knowledge and ways of doing things."*

To discover the unique giftings of each child, we as adults

need to experiment.

We need to observe.

We need to ask questions.

Years ago, I talked to Sajan George, the CEO of Matchbox Learning about how he transformed a bottom 10 percent performing Detroit public school into the top 10 percent in one school year. Sajan told me about an environment of experimentation. He described classrooms in which children are given over 10 different ways to engage with each material. For example, in learning fractions, a child may use a worksheet,

He could listen to audio examples.

He could use a pie graph manipulative.

He could use a baseball metric.

Humans are wired to learn. But we often get stuck on the method of delivery. Napoleon is credited with saying that there are no bad soldiers, only bad colonels. That's a sobering claim if we apply it to parents/teachers and children. How do we pull out the best in each child we encounter? I don't know... and neither will you, until you put aside preconceptions, ask questions, and enter the great and grand experiment that is life.

CHALLENGE #20

Think about one of your child's least favorite things to do. Now, without thinking about it too much, describe the first question that comes to your mind. Next, think of what you can do this week that will lead you into position not to answer the question, but to ask another. Our journey is not to find answers, but to find better questions.

Keep on learning

I hope that during these pages you've seen the value that comes from learning music with your child.

If I can leave you with one final thought.

You can do it!

Or, putting it in the words of Phil Knight and Nike, "Just Do It."

Everything that I've written in this book is achievable with or without a music education. It doesn't come free though. It requires an investment. But it's not money, or fancy instruments, or even the best teachers.

It's you.

Your child will thrive musically if you invest yourself personally into their art. Walk the road beside them, and at times you'll find yourself journeying side by side, while at others you'll need to carry them, and yet sometimes it may be they that give you a boost. But at some point, your journey will end, while theirs does not (cue: tears). And you will watch their footprints in the sand as they forge ahead. New adventures, wondrous delights, and beautiful music wafting through the air.

Christopher enjoyed a decade long career as a touring violinist with the Boston String Quartet. He is the founder of the School of Groove, Rock and Roll Daycare, and co-founder of Fiddlefox, a curriculum company which provides parents, children, and schools with musical content and resources from cultures around the world. All Fiddlefox materials are designed to be used by musicians and nonmusicians alike.

Learn more at **www.fiddlefoxmusic.com**

Made in USA - Kendallville, IN
44346_9781073322633
12 28 2021 2355